Baby's Photograph

*T*here is nothing quite like experiencing God's miracle of creation as you welcome your newborn into the world. The tiny hands, curled up toes, and velvety skin are a physical reminder of how fragile and wonderfully precious life really is.

Your baby's first year is an important time when you and your child begin to build a lifelong relationship based on mutual trust, love, understanding, and biblical principles. Each moment of this first year is a special event – from your baby's eager attempts at simple words to the day your child stands on wobbly little legs. Yet, with each day's busyness, the specifics of "when and where" – the unforgettable milestones – can be lost as other achievements quickly begin to mount up.

*The Miracle of Life: Baby's First Year* was created to capture these priceless moments in a beautifully designed record book. With delightful sections like Baby's Arrival, Bathtime and Water Play, First Christmas, and Plans and Prayers for the Future, you'll have a concise but thorough history of what is so often the most important year for a child. And years from now, or perhaps as an annual tradition together on your child's birthday, you'll be able to go back and read through this wonderful collection of memories, reliving each warm experience over and over again. God indeed does give us good things (Psalm 107:8-9) – and he wants us to joyfully celebrate them!

# The Miracle OF LIFE

*Baby's First Year*

## CONTENTS

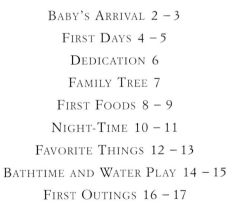

TYNDALE HOUSE PUBLISHERS, INC.
WHEATON, ILLINOIS

# —Baby's Arrival—

Date and day of birth

Place of birth

Time of birth

Weight at birth

Length at birth

Before I formed you in the
womb, I knew you.
Jeremiah 1:5 NIV

Color of eyes

Color of hair

Circumference of head

Name of Doctor

Description of the birth

*Baby's appearance*

*Birth cards received*

Every child born into the world
is a new thought of God,
an ever-fresh and radiant possibility.

Kate Douglas Wiggin

BABY'S FIRST PHOTOGRAPH

BIRTH ANNOUNCEMENT

# FIRST DAYS

First visitors

Their comments

Feeding schedule

Baby's feeding times

Duration of a feeding

Description of a feeding

Sleeping schedule

Sleeping times

Wakeful times

Favorite sleeping position

Mother's feelings

Father's feelings

HUSH MY DEAR, LIE STILL AND SLUMBER,
HOLY ANGELS GUARD THY BED.
HEAVENLY BLESSINGS WITHOUT NUMBER
GENTLY FALLING ON THY HEAD.

Isaac Watts, *A Cradle Hymn*

Flowers received

PHOTOGRAPH

Gifts received

From whom

# DEDICATION

INVITATION

Gifts received

Your baby's behavior

Your baby's outfit

Description of ceremony

Scripture read

I PRAYED FOR THIS CHILD, SO NOW
I GIVE HIM TO THE LORD.

1 Samuel 1:27-28 NIV

Special guests

# FAMILY TREE

### Maternal

**Great-Grandmother**
....................................
....................................
....................................

**Great-Grandfather**
....................................
....................................

**Great-Grandmother**
....................................
....................................
....................................

**Great-Grandfather**
....................................
....................................

**Grandmother**
....................................
....................................

**Grandfather**
....................................
....................................

**Mother**
....................................

### Paternal

**Great-Grandmother**
....................................
....................................
....................................

**Great-Grandfather**
....................................
....................................

**Great-Grandmother**
....................................
....................................
....................................

**Great-Grandfather**
....................................
....................................

**Grandmother**
....................................
....................................

**Grandfather**
....................................
....................................

**Father**
....................................

**Sisters**
....................................

**Baby**
....................................

**Brothers**
....................................

# FIRST FOODS

Most babies are introduced to solid foods at between three and six months old,
and will relish discovering new tastes and textures.

H E GIVES FOOD TO THOSE WHO TRUST HIM;
HE ALWAYS REMEMBERS HIS COVENANT.

Psalm 111:5 NLT

*God is great and God is good,
And we thank him for our food;
By his hand we are all fed,
Give us, Lord, our daily bread. Amen.*

Date your baby first:

*Ate puréed food*

*Ate solid food*

*Ate with a spoon*

*Ate in a high chair*

*Drank from a cup*

*Thank-you for the world so sweet,
Thank-you for the food we eat,
Thank-you for the birds that sing,
Thank-you, Lord, for everything. Amen.*

*Favorite food*

*Description of a meal*

*Date of weaning*

# TEETHING

A<small>DAM AND</small> E<small>VE HAD MANY ADVANTAGES, BUT THE PRINCIPAL ONE WAS THAT THEY ESCAPED TEETHING.</small>

Mark Twain

A baby cuts 20 primary or milk teeth, which begin to be replaced with permanent teeth when the child is about six years old. The appearance of the first tooth is a milestone in a baby's life, although it can cause a great deal of discomfort. Some babies find chewing on a teething ring soothes the gums and helps lessen the pain.

*Date of first tooth*

*Date of second tooth*

*Date of third tooth*

*Date of fourth tooth*

*Date of fifth tooth*

*Teething symptoms*

*Notes*

Top teeth

Teething order

Bottom teeth

# NIGHT-TIME

CHILDREN ARE A GIFT FROM THE LORD; THEY ARE A REWARD FROM HIM.

Psalm 127:3 NLT

Bedtime ...........................................................

Favorite sleeping position ...........................................................

Wakes at ...........................................................

Bedtime comforters ...........................................................

First sleeps through night ...........................................................

First sleeps in crib ...........................................................

Now I lay me down to sleep
In my Father's tender care.
I pray for quiet, soothing rest,
And sweetest dreams of
my Savior fair.

JESUS LOVES ME, THIS I KNOW
FOR THE BIBLE TELLS ME SO
LITTLE ONES TO HIM BELONG
THEY ARE WEAK, BUT HE IS STRONG.

Anna B. Warner

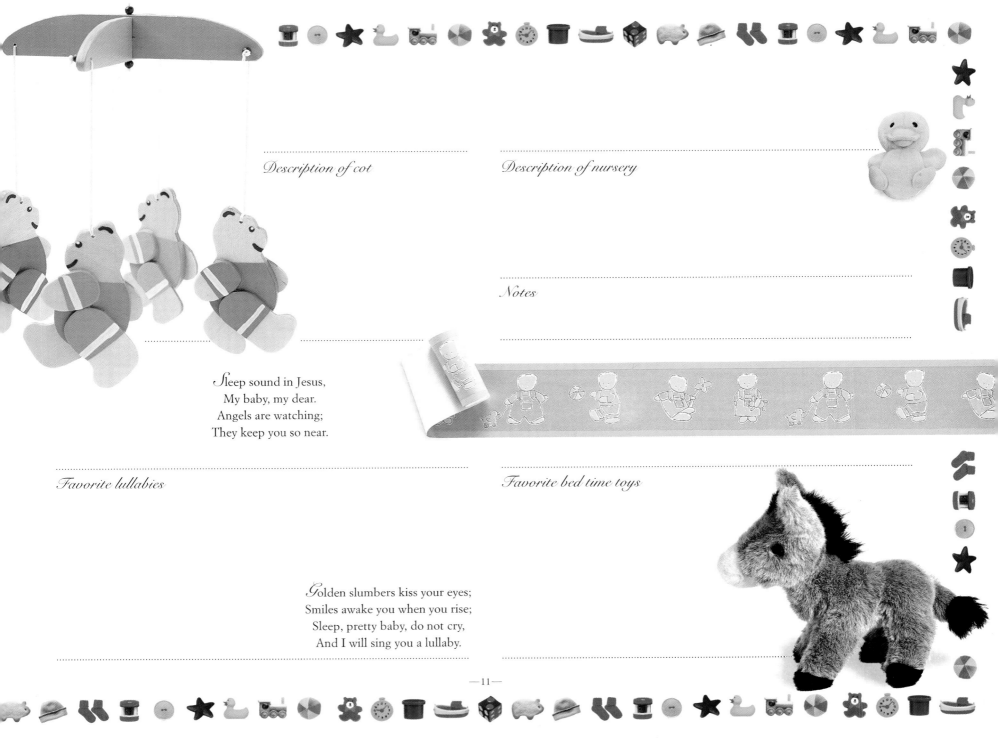

Description of cot

Description of nursery

Notes

Sleep sound in Jesus,
My baby, my dear.
Angels are watching;
They keep you so near.

Favorite lullabies

Favorite bed time toys

Golden slumbers kiss your eyes;
Smiles awake you when you rise;
Sleep, pretty baby, do not cry,
And I will sing you a lullaby.

# FAVORITE THINGS

Your baby's favorite:

........................................................    ........................................

*Mobile*

GOD RICHLY PROVIDES US WITH EVERYTHING
FOR OUR ENJOYMENT.

1 Timothy 6:17 NIV

....................................    *Toys*

.................................................................................

........................................................    .................................

*Pictures*

.................................................................................

........................................................    .................................

*Books*    *Cuddly toys*

.................................................................................

........................................................

*Objects*

.................................................................................

........................................................    .................................

Games

Activities

Sounds

Words

People

Animals

Stories

Songs and Nursery Rhymes

ALL THINGS BRIGHT AND BEAUTIFUL,
ALL CREATURES, GREAT AND SMALL,
ALL THINGS WISE AND WONDERFUL,
THE LORD GOD MADE THEM ALL.

Cecil Frances Alexander

*First enjoys bath*

*First time in a big bathtub*

*Response to being bathed*

*Response to hair being washed*

LET THE HEAD GROW WISE,
BUT KEEP THE HEART ALWAYS
YOUNG AND PLAYFUL.
David Livingstone

*Favorite bath toys*

*Bathtime activities*

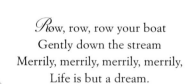

Row, row, row your boat
Gently down the stream
Merrily, merrily, merrily, merrily,
Life is but a dream.

One, two, three, four, five,
Once I caught a fish alive,
Six, seven, eight, nine, ten,
Then I let him go again.
Why did you let him go?
Because he bit my finger so.
Which finger did he bite?
This little finger on the right.

First water play in garden

First play in wading pool

First swim in swimming pool

Your baby's swimwear

PHOTOGRAPH

Favorite water games

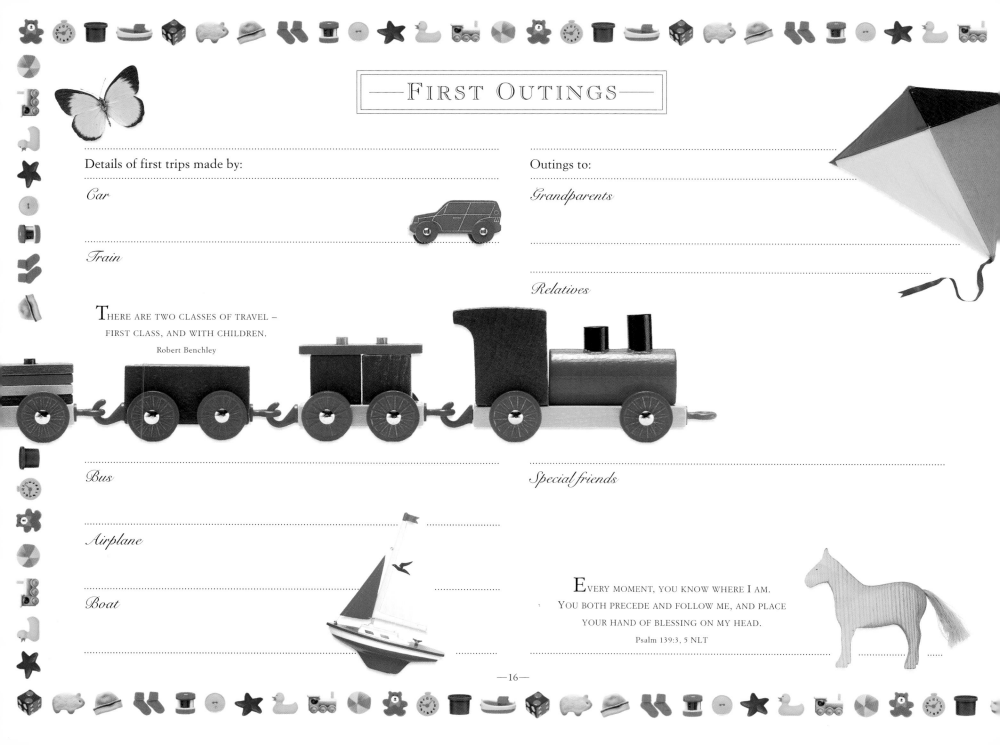

# FIRST OUTINGS

Details of first trips made by:

Car

Train

Bus

Airplane

Boat

THERE ARE TWO CLASSES OF TRAVEL –
FIRST CLASS, AND WITH CHILDREN.
Robert Benchley

Outings to:

Grandparents

Relatives

Special friends

E VERY MOMENT, YOU KNOW WHERE I AM.
YOU BOTH PRECEDE AND FOLLOW ME, AND PLACE
YOUR HAND OF BLESSING ON MY HEAD.
Psalm 139:3, 5 NLT

Outings to:

*Parks and playgrounds*

*Beaches or cities*

*The countryside*

*Church*

GOD MADE LIFE A LITTLE LIGHT,
WITHIN THE WORLD TO GLOW;
A TINY FLAME THAT BURNETH BRIGHT,
WHEREVER I MAY GO.
M. Bentham-Edwards

*Notes*

PHOTOGRAPH

# FIRST CHRISTMAS

F OR TO US A CHILD IS BORN,
TO US A SON IS GIVEN.

Isaiah 9:6 NIV

Christmas Day:

*Where it was spent*

*Who it was spent with*

*Your present to your baby*

*Stocking gifts*

*Gifts received*

*From whom*

*Description of the holidays*

*A*way in a manger,
no crib for a bed,
The little Lord Jesus
laid down His sweet head;
The stars in the sky
looked down where he lay,
The little Lord Jesus,
asleep on the hay.

Christmas Eve:

*Where it was spent*

*Who it was spent with*

*Description of Christmas Eve*

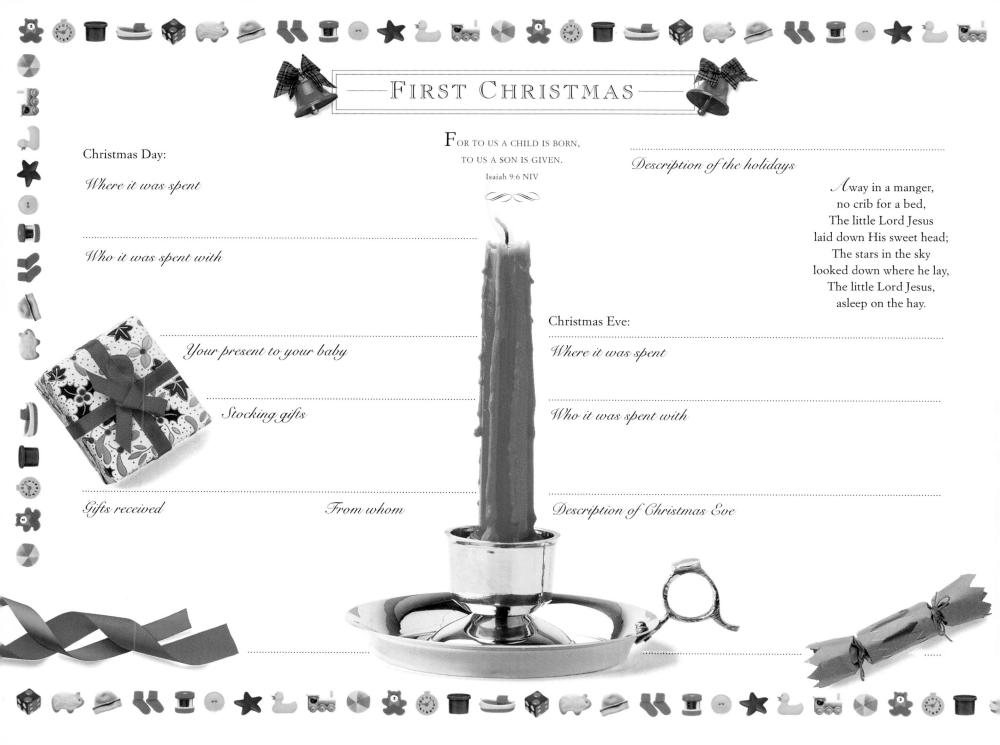

*Favorite Christmas presents*

*Family Christmas activities*

*Favorite Christmas games*

*Description of the Christmas tree*

PHOTOGRAPH

*Christmas weather*

*Notes*

# First Vacation

Date

Place

Who was there

Travel details

Accommodation

Favorite activities

Favorite outings

Baby's behavior

Baby's new friends

PHOTOGRAPH

*Favorite memories of the vacation*

Iᴛ ɪs ᴀ ʜᴀᴘᴘʏ ᴛᴀʟᴇɴᴛ ᴛᴏ ᴋɴᴏᴡ ʜᴏᴡ ᴛᴏ ᴘʟᴀʏ.

Ralph Waldo Emerson

# FIRST BIRTHDAY

Date ....................................................

How celebrated ....................................................

Who was there ....................................................

1

Description of cake ....................................................

Your baby's outfit ....................................................

Gifts received ....................................................

YOU ARE PRECIOUS AND
HONORED IN MY SIGHT,
AND I LOVE YOU.
Isaiah 43:4 NIV

Your present ....................................................

*Your baby's behavior*

*H*appy birthday to you
Happy birthday to you
Happy birthday dear baby
Happy birthday to you.

PHOTOGRAPH

*Notes*

# MILESTONES

A CHILD MORE THAN ALL OTHER GIFTS
THAT GOD CAN OFFER TO MAN
BRINGS HOPE WITH IT, AND
FORWARD-LOOKING THOUGHTS.

William Wordsworth

First smiles

First discovers hands and feet

First grasps object

First holds head up

First sits up

First kiss

First haircut

First solid food

First tooth

First crawls

First stands

First steps

First waves goodbye

First words

First says Mama

First says Dada

—24—

*W*E FIND DELIGHT IN THE BEAUTY AND
HAPPINESS OF CHILDREN THAT MAKES THE
HEART TOO BIG FOR THE BODY.
Ralph Waldo Emerson

First recognizes:

*Mother*

*Father*

*Grandparents*

*Special friends*

*Animals*

*First friends*

PHOTOGRAPH

*Notes*

# Mementos

Identification tag from hospital

Footprints

Handprints

PARENTS ARE GARDENERS – PLANTING THE SEEDS OF FAITH, TRUTH, AND LOVE THAT DEVELOP INTO THE FAIREST FLOWERS OF CHARACTER, VIRTUE, AND HAPPINESS IN THE LIVES OF THEIR CHILDREN.

J. Harold Gwynne

*Lock of hair*

*Special treasures*

# MEDICAL RECORD

THE LORD WILL GUIDE YOU CONTINUALLY, WATERING YOUR LIFE
WHEN YOU ARE DRY AND KEEPING YOU HEALTHY, TOO.

Isaiah 58:11 NLT

| Immunization details | | | Illnesses | | |
| --- | --- | --- | --- | --- | --- |
| *Vaccine* | *Age* | *Date* | *Diagnosis* | *Age* | *Date* |
| *Diphtheria | Tetanus | Pertussis* | | | | | |
| *Polio* | | | | | |
| *Hemophilus b* | | | | | |
| *Measles | Mumps | Rubella* | | | | | |
| *Other* | | | | | |

Visits to doctor

| Reason | Age | Date |
| --- | --- | --- |
| | | |

Allergies

Blood group

Eyesight test

Hearing test

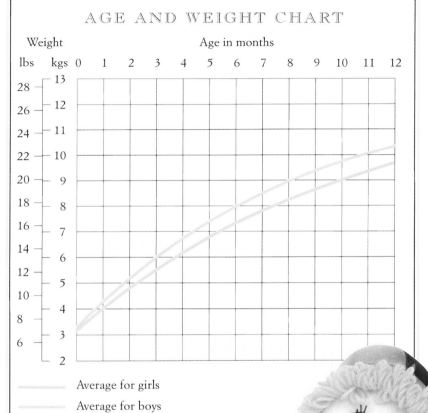

## AGE AND WEIGHT CHART

Weight                                    Age in months

| lbs | kgs | 0 | 1 | 2 | 3 | 4 | 5 | 6 | 7 | 8 | 9 | 10 | 11 | 12 |
| --- | --- | --- | --- | --- | --- | --- | --- | --- | --- | --- | --- | --- | --- | --- |
| 28 | 13 | | | | | | | | | | | | | |
| 26 | 12 | | | | | | | | | | | | | |
| 24 | 11 | | | | | | | | | | | | | |
| 22 | 10 | | | | | | | | | | | | | |
| 20 | 9 | | | | | | | | | | | | | |
| 18 | 8 | | | | | | | | | | | | | |
| 16 | 7 | | | | | | | | | | | | | |
| 14 | 6 | | | | | | | | | | | | | |
| 12 | 5 | | | | | | | | | | | | | |
| 10 | 4 | | | | | | | | | | | | | |
| 8 | | | | | | | | | | | | | | |
| 6 | 3 | | | | | | | | | | | | | |
| | 2 | | | | | | | | | | | | | |

——— Average for girls

——— Average for boys

Notes

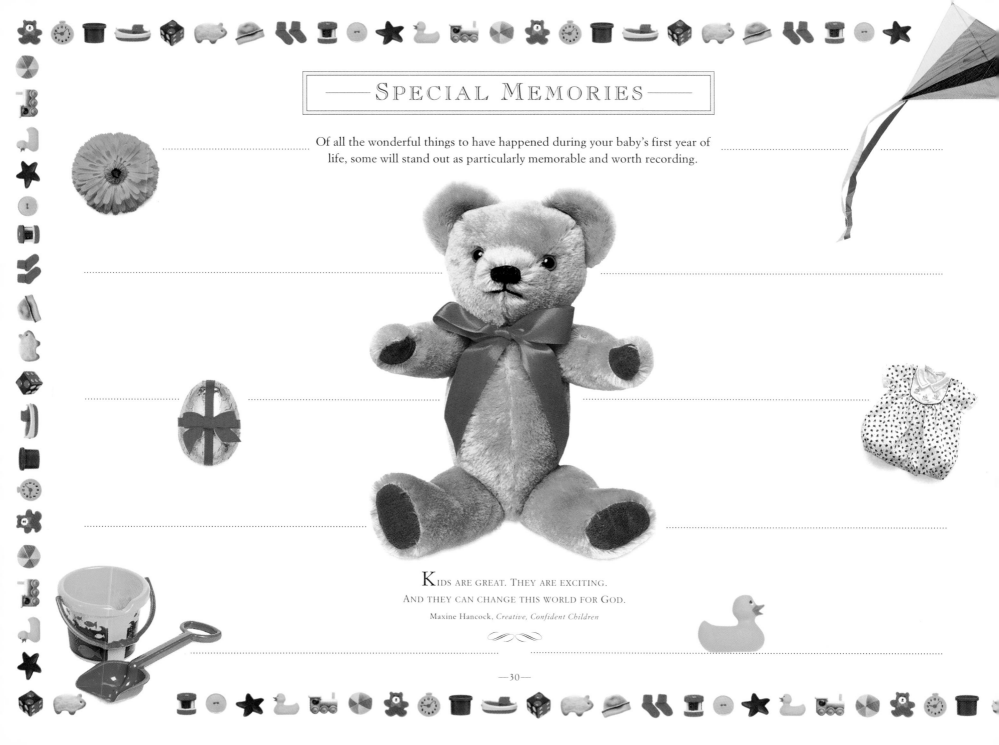

# SPECIAL MEMORIES

Of all the wonderful things to have happened during your baby's first year of life, some will stand out as particularly memorable and worth recording.

KIDS ARE GREAT. THEY ARE EXCITING.
AND THEY CAN CHANGE THIS WORLD FOR GOD.

Maxine Hancock, *Creative, Confident Children*

—30—

# PLANS AND PRAYERS
## FOR THE FUTURE

Dreams for your baby

Possible schools

Character traits & skills you've noticed

Prayers for your baby's future

"For I know the plans I have for you," declares the
Lord, "plans to give you hope and a future."

Jeremiah 29:11 NIV

PHOTOGRAPH

# MONTH 1

FROM TO

| DAY 1 | DAY 2 | DAY 3 | DAY 4 | | DAY 5 | DAY 6 |
|---|---|---|---|---|---|---|
| Date............ | | | | | | |
| DAY 7 | DAY 8 | DAY 9 | DAY 10 | DAY 11 | DAY 12 | DAY 13 |
| DAY 14 | DAY 15 | DAY 16 | DAY 17 | DAY 18 | DAY 19 | DAY 20 |
| | DAY 21 | DAY 22 | DAY 23 | DAY 24 | DAY 25 | DAY 26 |
| | DAY 27 | DAY 28 | DAY 29 | DAY 30 | DAY 31 | |

# MONTH 1

FROM                    TO.

Weight

Length

Sleeping pattern

Bedtime

Feeding pattern

Physical changes

Medical checkups

New sounds

PHOTOGRAPH

Date of photograph

A typical day

Response to mother

Response to father

—33—

FROM .................................... TO ....................................

PHOTOGRAPH

Weight .............................

Length .............................

Sleeping pattern .............................
.............................

Bedtime .............................

Feeding pattern .............................

Physical changes .............................
.............................

Medical checkups .............................
.............................

New sounds .............................

Date of photograph .............................

A typical day

Response to mother
.............................

Response to father
.............................

FROM                    TO

| DAY 1 | DAY 2 | DAY 3 | DAY 4 | DAY 5 | DAY 6 | DAY 7 |
| Date............... | | | | | | |
| DAY 8 | DAY 9 | DAY 10 | DAY 11 | DAY 12 | DAY 13 | DAY 14 |
| DAY 15 | DAY 16 | DAY 17 | | DAY 18 | DAY 19 | DAY 20 |
| DAY 21 | DAY 22 | DAY 23 | DAY 24 | DAY 25 | DAY 26 | |
| DAY 27 | DAY 28 | DAY 29 | DAY 30 | DAY 31 | | |

FROM ............................. TO .............................

| DAY 1 | DAY 2 | DAY 3 | DAY 4 | DAY 5 | DAY 6 | DAY 7 |
| Date........................... | | | | | | |
| DAY 8 | DAY 9 | DAY 10 | DAY 11 | DAY 12 | DAY 13 |
| DAY 14 | DAY 15 | DAY 16 | DAY 17 | DAY 18 | DAY 19 | DAY 20 |
| DAY 21 | DAY 22 | DAY 23 | DAY 24 | DAY 25 | DAY 26 |
| DAY 27 | DAY 28 | DAY 29 | DAY 30 | DAY 31 |

FROM _____ TO _____

Weight _____ Length _____

Sleeping pattern _____

Wakes up _____

Bedtime _____

Feeding pattern _____

Medical checkups _____

Physical changes _____

New sounds _____

Response to mother _____

Response to father _____

A typical day _____

PHOTOGRAPH

Date of photograph

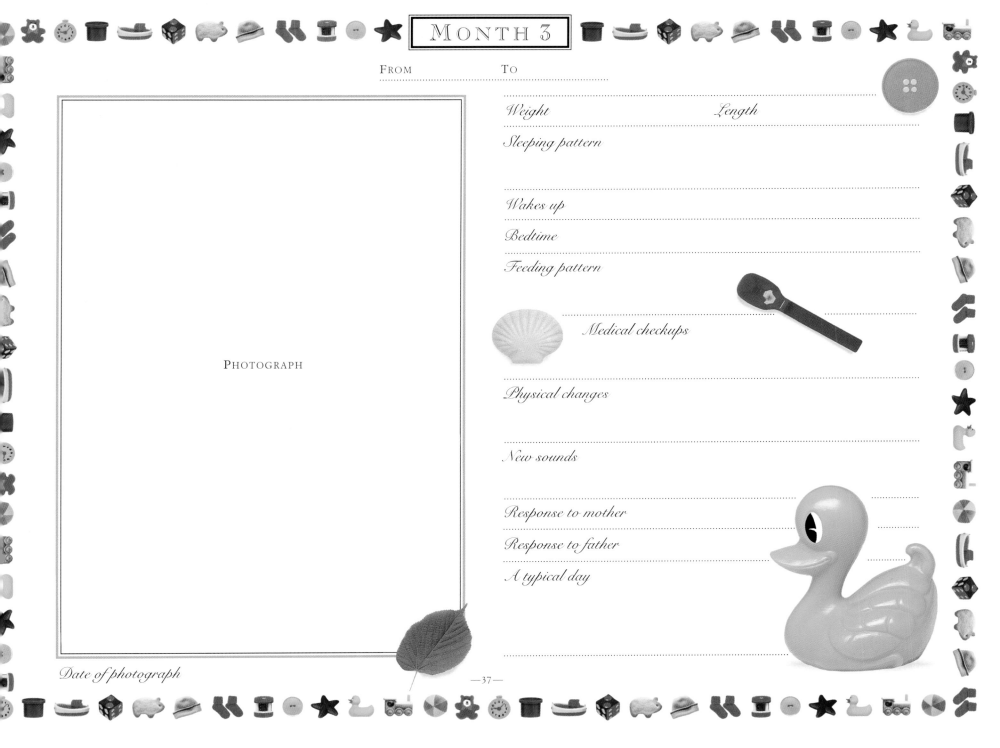

FROM                    TO

Weight                    Length

Sleeping pattern

Wakes up

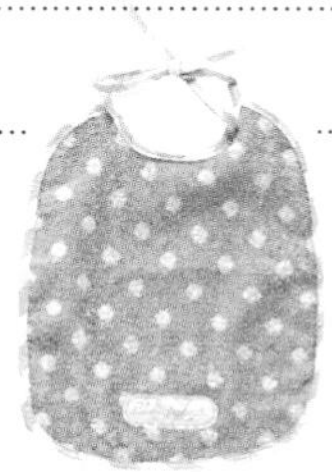

Bedtime

Description of mealtime

Physical changes

New movements

New sounds

Medical checkups

Favorite activities

A typical day

PHOTOGRAPH

Date of photograph

FROM ............... TO ...............

DAY 1
Date........................

DAY 2

DAY 3

DAY 4

DAY 5

DAY 6

DAY 7

DAY 8

DAY 9

DAY 10

DAY 11

DAY 12

DAY 13

DAY 14

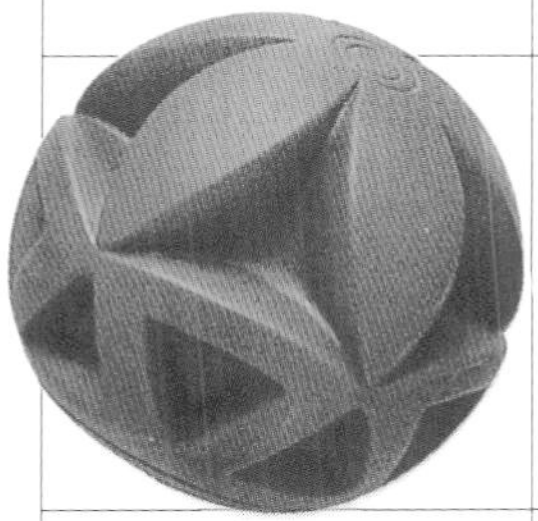

DAY 15

DAY 16

DAY 17

DAY 18

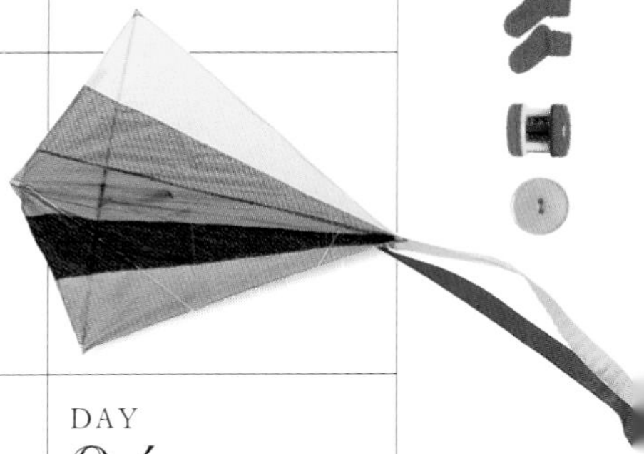

DAY 19

DAY 20

DAY 21

DAY 22

DAY 23

DAY 24

DAY 25

DAY 26

DAY 27

DAY 28

DAY 29

DAY 30

DAY 31

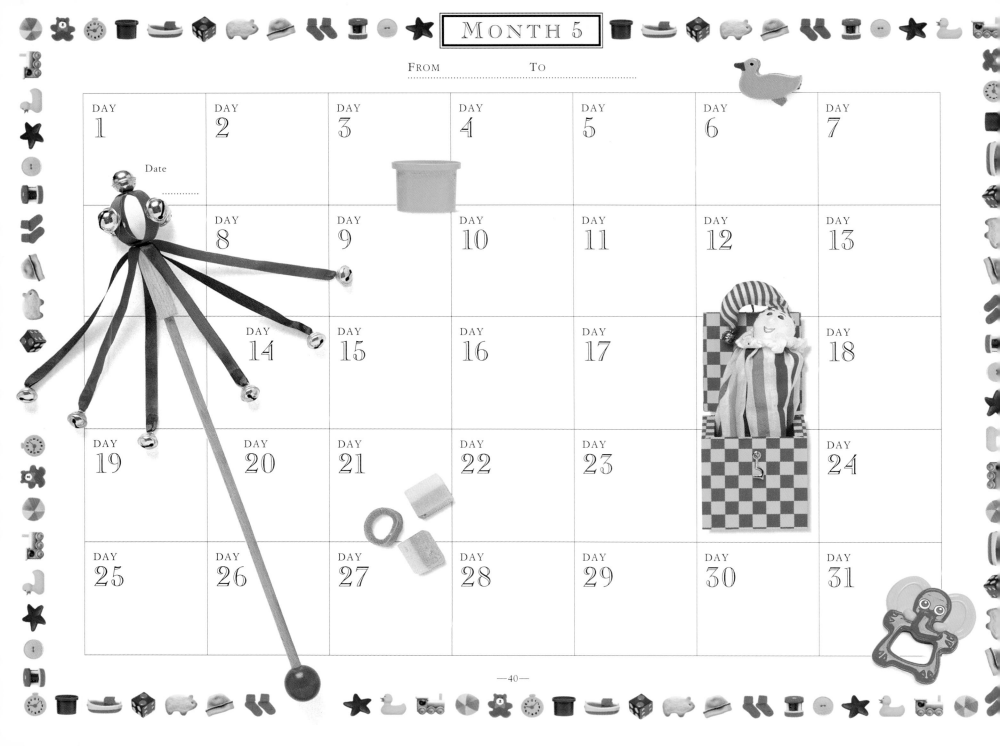

FROM     TO
...............................................................

| DAY 1 | DAY 2 | DAY 3 | DAY 4 | DAY 5 | DAY 6 | DAY 7 |
|---|---|---|---|---|---|---|
| Date ............. | DAY 8 | DAY 9 | DAY 10 | DAY 11 | DAY 12 | DAY 13 |
| | DAY 14 | DAY 15 | DAY 16 | DAY 17 | | DAY 18 |
| DAY 19 | DAY 20 | DAY 21 | DAY 22 | DAY 23 | | DAY 24 |
| DAY 25 | DAY 26 | DAY 27 | DAY 28 | DAY 29 | DAY 30 | DAY 31 |

FROM ................................. TO .................................

Weight .................................

Length .................................

Sleeping pattern .................................

.................................

Wakes up .................................

Bedtime .................................

Description of mealtime .................................

.................................

.................................

Favorite foods .................................

.................................

Medical checkups .................................

.................................

PHOTOGRAPH

Date of photograph .................................

New movements .................................

Favorite outing .................................

Physical changes .................................

A typical day .................................

New sounds .................................

Favorite activities .................................

FROM ........................ TO ........................

PHOTOGRAPH

Weight ........................................

Length ........................................

Sleeping pattern ........................................
........................................

Wakes up ........................................

Bedtime ........................................

Description of mealtime ........................................
........................................
........................................

Favorite foods ........................................
........................................

Medical checkups ........................................

Date of photograph ........................................

Favorite outing ........................................

A typical day ........................................
........................................

New movements ........................................

Physical changes ........................................

New sounds ........................................

Favorite activities ........................................

FROM ............................ TO ............................

| | | | | | |
|---|---|---|---|---|---|
| DAY 1 <br> Date......................... | DAY 2 | DAY 3 | DAY 4 | DAY 5 | DAY 6 |
| DAY 7 | DAY 8 | DAY 9 | DAY 10 | DAY 11 | DAY 12 | DAY 13 |
| DAY 14 | DAY 15 | DAY 16 | DAY 17 | DAY 18 | DAY 19 | DAY 20 |
| DAY 21 | DAY 22 | | DAY 23 | DAY 24 | DAY 25 |
| DAY 26 | DAY 27 | DAY 28 | DAY 29 | DAY 30 | DAY 31 |

FROM .................... TO ....................

DAY 1

Date....................

DAY 2

DAY 3

DAY 4

DAY 5

DAY 6

DAY 7

DAY 8

DAY 9

DAY 10

DAY 11

DAY 12

DAY 13

DAY 14

DAY 15

DAY 16

DAY 17

DAY 18

DAY 19

DAY 20

DAY 21

DAY 22

DAY 23

DAY 24

DAY 25

DAY 26

DAY 27

DAY 28

DAY 29

DAY 30

DAY 31

FROM .......... TO ..........

Weight

Length

Sleeping pattern

Wakes up

Bedtime

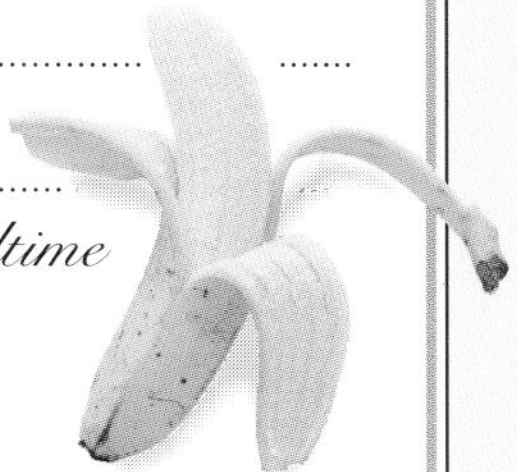

Description of mealtime

Favorite foods

Medical checkups

New movements

Physical changes

New sounds

Favorite activities

PHOTOGRAPH

Date of photograph

Favorite outing

A typical day

—45—

FROM ........................ TO ........................

PHOTOGRAPH

Weight .........................................

Length .........................................

Sleeping pattern .........................................

Wakes up .........................................

Bedtime .........................................

Description of mealtime .........................................

Favorite foods .........................................

Medical checkups .........................................

Date of photograph .........................................

Favorite outing .........................................

A typical day .........................................

New movements .........................................

Physical changes .........................................

New sounds .........................................

Favorite activities .........................................

FROM          TO

DAY 1

Date............

DAY 2

DAY 3

DAY 4

DAY 5

DAY 6

DAY 7

DAY 8

DAY 9

DAY 10

DAY 11

DAY 12

DAY 13

DAY 14

DAY 15

DAY 16

DAY 17

DAY 18

DAY 19

DAY 20

DAY 21

DAY 22

DAY 23

DAY 24

DAY 25

DAY 26

DAY 27

DAY 28

DAY 29

DAY 30

DAY 31

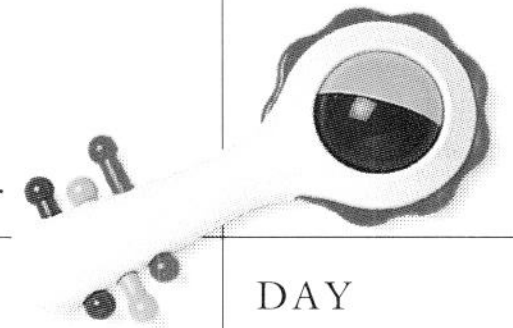

# MONTH 9

FROM       TO

......................................................

| DAY 1 | DAY 2 | DAY 3 | DAY 4 | DAY 5 | DAY 6 |
|---|---|---|---|---|---|
| Date.................. | | | | | |
| DAY 7 | DAY 8 | DAY 9 | DAY 10 | DAY 11 | DAY 12 | DAY 13 |
| DAY 14 | DAY 15 | DAY 16 | DAY 17 | DAY 18 | DAY 19 | DAY 20 |
| | | | DAY 21 | DAY 22 | DAY 23 | DAY 24 | DAY 25 |
| | DAY 26 | DAY 27 | DAY 28 | DAY 29 | DAY 30 | DAY 31 |

FROM .................................... TO ....................................

..........................................................................................

Weight ........................... Length ...........................

Sleeping pattern ...........................................................

..........................................................................................

Wakes up ..........................................................................

Bedtime ..............................................................................

Description of mealtime .............................................

..........................................................................................

Physical changes ............................................................

..........................................................................................

New movements ...............................................................

..........................................................................................

New sounds .........................................................................

..........................................................................................

Medical checkups ...........................................................

Favorite activities ..........................................................

..........................................................................................

A typical day .....................................................................

..........................................................................................

PHOTOGRAPH

Date of photograph

FROM ................................... TO ...................................

Weight ............................. Length .............................

Sleeping pattern
..................................................................

..................................................................

Wakes up ...........................................

Bedtime ...........................................

Description of mealtime .............................

..................................................................

Physical changes ...................................

New movements
..................................................................

..................................................................

New sounds
..................................................................

Medical checkups ...................................

Favorite activities
..................................................................

A typical day
..................................................................

PHOTOGRAPH

Date of photograph

FROM           TO

DAY
1

Date..............................

DAY
2

DAY
3

DAY
4

DAY
5

DAY
6

DAY
7

DAY
8

DAY
9

DAY
10

DAY
11

DAY
12

DAY
13

DAY
14

DAY
15

DAY
16

DAY
17

DAY
18

DAY
19

DAY
20

DAY
21

DAY
22

DAY
23

DAY
24

DAY
25

DAY
26

DAY
27

DAY
28

DAY
29

DAY
30

DAY
31

FROM          TO
................................................................

| DAY 1 | DAY 2 | DAY 3 | DAY 4 | DAY 5 | DAY 6 | DAY 7 |
|---|---|---|---|---|---|---|
| Date........................ | | | | | | |
| DAY 8 | DAY 9 | DAY 10 | DAY 11 | DAY 12 | DAY 12 | DAY 13 |
| DAY 14 | DAY 15 | DAY 16 | DAY 17 | DAY 18 | DAY 19 | DAY 20 |
| DAY 21 | DAY 22 | DAY 23 | DAY 24 | DAY 25 | DAY 26 | |
| | DAY 27 | DAY 28 | DAY 29 | DAY 30 | DAY 31 | |

FROM ............................ TO ............................

Weight ............................

Length ............................

Sleeping pattern ............................
............................

Wakes up ............................

Bedtime ............................

Description of mealtime ............................
............................
............................

Favorite foods ............................
............................

Medical checkups ............................

New movements ............................

Physical changes ............................

New sounds ............................

Favorite activities ............................

PHOTOGRAPH

Date of photograph ............................

Favorite outing ............................

A typical day ............................
............................

FROM ............................ TO ............................

PHOTOGRAPH

Weight ....................................

Length ....................................

Sleeping pattern ....................................

....................................

Wakes up ....................................

Bedtime ....................................

Description of mealtime ....................................

Favorite foods ....................................

....................................

Medical checkups ....................................

Date of photograph ....................................

Favorite outing ....................................

A typical day ....................................

New movements ....................................

Physical changes ....................................

New sounds ....................................

Favorite activities ....................................

FROM ........................ TO ........................

| DAY 1 | DAY 2 | DAY 3 | DAY 4 | DAY 5 | DAY 6 |
| Date.................... | | | | | |
| DAY 7 | DAY 8 | DAY 9 | DAY 10 | DAY 11 | DAY 12 | DAY 13 |
| DAY 14 | DAY 15 | | DAY 16 | DAY 17 | DAY 18 | DAY 19 |
| DAY 20 | DAY 21 | DAY 22 | DAY 23 | DAY 24 | | DAY 25 |
| DAY 26 | DAY 27 | DAY 28 | DAY 29 | DAY 30 | | DAY 31 |

A Dorling Kindersley book

*Design* Bernard Higton

First published in Great Britain in 1995 by
Dorling Kindersley Limited,
9 Henrietta Street, London WC2E 8PS

All Scripture quotations, unless otherwise indicated, are
taken from the Holy Bible, New International Version®.
NIV®. Copyright © 1973, 1978, 1984 by International
Bible Society. Used by permission of Zondervan
Publishing House. All rights reserved.

Scripture quotations marked NLT are taken from the
Holy Bible, New Living Translation, copyright © 1996.
Used by permission of Tyndale House Publishers, Inc.,
Wheaton, Illinois 60189. All rights reserved.

This edition published in the United States by
Tyndale House Publishers, Inc.
351 Executive Drive
Carol Stream, Illinois 60188

Visit Tyndale's exciting Web site at www.tyndale.com

ISBN 0-8423-3651-6

Color reproduction by Colourscan, Singapore
Printed and bound in by Tien Wah Press, Singapore

04 03 02 01 00 99 98
8 7 6 5 4 3 2 1